WE COME FROM

South Africa

ALISON BROWNLIE

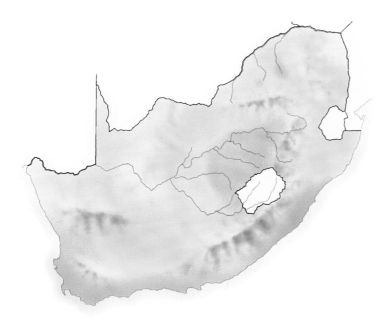

HODDER
Wayland

an imprint of Hodder Children's Books

WE COME FROM

China • France • Germany
India • Jamaica • Japan
Nigeria • South Africa

Many of the people you are about to meet live in a township in South Africa called Soweto. Like any country, South Africa has many different types of lifestyles. People live in the countryside as well as in towns and cities.

Cover: Tshepo and his friends have a bicycle which they share between them.
Title page (from top to bottom): The rugged coast of the Western Cape; traditional tribal food preparation in a village; a wild white rhino in a game park; Johannesburg city centre; one of South Africa's many gold mines.
Contents page: Black and white children playing cricket together.
Index: At weekends, Tshepo meets his friends at the playground.

All Wayland books encourage children to read and help them improve their literacy.

✓ The contents page, page numbers, headings and index help locate specific pieces of information.

✓ The glossary reinforces alphabetic knowledge and extends vocabulary.

✓ The further information section suggests other books dealing with the same subject.

Series editor: Katie Orchard
Book editor: Phillippa Smith
Designer: Jean Wheeler
Production controller: Tracy Fewtrell

Acknowledgements: All the photographs in this book were taken by Gordon Clements, but thanks go also to Thomas Chauke, photographer with the Office of the Premier, Gauteng Province, for his invaluable assistance.

The map artwork on page 5 was produced by Peter Bull.

First published in Great Britain in 1999 by Wayland Publishers Ltd.
This paperback edition published in 2002 by Hodder Wayland, an imprint of Hodder Children's Books
Reprinted in 2005

© Hodder Wayland 1999

Hodder Children's Books
A division of Hodder Headline Limited
338 Euston Road, London NW1 3BH

British Library Cataloguing in Publication Data
Brownlie, Alison
 We come from South Africa
1.South Africa - Geography - Juvenile literature
2.South Africa - Social conditions - 1961 - Juvenile literature
I.Title II. South Africa
968'.065

ISBN 0 7502 4363 5

Typeset by Jean Wheeler, England
Printed and bound in China

Contents

Welcome to South Africa!

'My name is Tshepo. This is me with my mother and father and my big sister, Mathapelo, who is eleven.'

Tshepo is seven years old. He lives with his parents and older sister in Soweto, a township on the edge of Johannesburg. Johannesburg is one of the largest cities in South Africa. You can see where Johannesburg is on the map on page 5.

▲ From left to right: Mathapelo, Mr Mohasoane, Tshepo and Mrs Mohasoane.

▲ South Africa's place in the world.

▼ This book takes you to Soweto, as well as the rest of South Africa.

Pronunciation guide

	you say:
Tshepo	Sheppo
Mathapelo	Matta-pello
Mohasoane	Mohar-so-warnay
Soweto	Swetto
Afrikaans	Afri-karns
Sotho	Sotto

SOUTH AFRICA

Capital cities	Cape Town and Pretoria
Land area	1.2 million square kilometres
Population	44 million people (80% are black people)
Main languages	English and Afrikaans and nine tribal languages including Zulu, Xhosa, Tswana and Sotho
Main religion	Christianity

The Land and Weather

South Africa is a big country. More than half the people live in large cities. Many people leave the countryside looking for work in the cities.

▶ *Playing jumbo chess in a city park in Johannesburg.*

▼ *The flat veld farmland is good for growing wheat.*

The Drakensberg Mountains in the east of South Africa are the highest and wettest parts of the country. In the centre there is a large area of land called the veld. This is a high, fairly flat plateau. Further west again the land is lower and drier. In places it is almost a desert.

▲ *Its flat top has given this mountain the name of 'Table Mountain'. It is a famous tourist attraction near Cape Town.*

◄ *Many wild animals live in South Africa's game parks. As well as lions like this, there are elephants, zebra, leopards, monkeys, hippopotami and many others.*

Look at the map on page 5 and you will see that South Africa has a long coastline. It has many beautiful beaches.

Summers are usually hot and winters are mild. It is unusual for it to snow in South Africa, even on the high mountain tops.

▼ *One of South Africa's beautiful sandy beaches.*

'In the summer, when it is hot and dry, I help my dad water the garden.' Tshepo.

9

At Home

A few years ago South Africa had strict laws to keep black and white people apart. They could not even use the same public toilet. This was known as Apartheid.

As a result of Apartheid, there are huge differences between the lives of white and black. White people are usually richer than black people.

▲ Tshepo likes skipping in his garden.

◀ In many parts of Soweto people build their homes from recycled materials.

▶ These luxury houses are in Johannesburg.

However Tshepo's family is quite well off. They live in a bungalow with a small garden. Their house has a kitchen, a living room, a bathroom and three bedrooms. They have a colour TV, a midi hi-fi system and a microwave.

▲ *Children playing outside a block of flats in Cape Town.*

'I've got lots of coloured pencils and I like drawing and colouring' Tshepo.

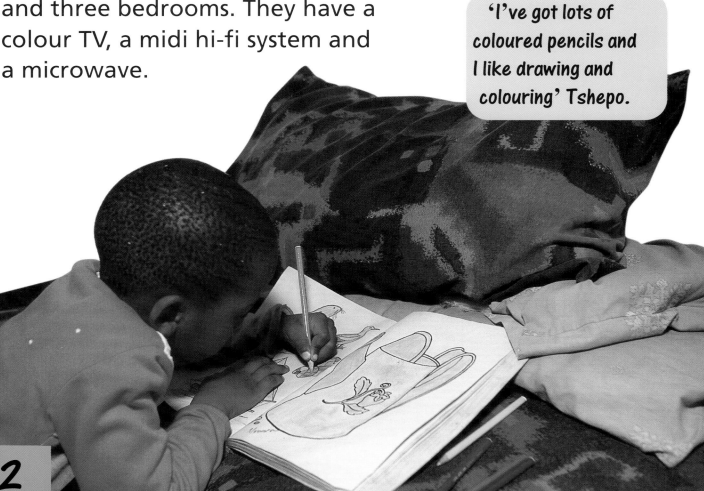

◀ Some homes do not have running water, so families collect it in metal drums or plastic containers.

In the countryside people live on farms or in small villages. People collect water from a well and only a very few have electricity. In the cities the larger houses have swimming pools and wealthier families employ maids to do the housework.

▼ In villages, many jobs are done outside, in the shade of a tree.

13

Food and Cooking

Most people who live in the country villages grow vegetables for themselves. They grow potatoes, onions and different kinds of cabbages. The food is often prepared and cooked outdoors.

In the countryside there are large modern farms that raise cattle, sheep and goats. Most people like to eat meat and barbecues are very popular. Sometimes the meat is cut into strips and dried. This is called *biltong*.

▲ *Barbecues are called* braai *in South Africa .*

▶ *On small farms people do most of the work by hand.*

'Porridge is my favourite food.' Tshepo.

14

◄ There are many different vegetables for sale in a city market.

Wheat and maize grow well on the veld. People like to eat a type of porridge made from maize.

South Africa has a good climate for growing fruit such as oranges and apples. These are often sold to other countries. In the cities people enjoy eating out in restaurants.

▶ In Tshepo's house his mum does most of the cooking.

◄ Sifting the corn meal, or 'mealie', to make porridge.

17

At Work

Many people in the countryside work as farmers growing the food they need. Some move to the cities to find work in offices and on building sites.

▼ *Some people work in the game parks looking after the wild animals.*

▲ *Many women in cities work in factories making clothes.*

18

South Africa produces more gold and diamonds than any other country, and there are many jobs as miners.

Both Tshepo's parents work for the government. His mother works as a secretary.

'I work in a chemistry laboratory. I check that factories are not causing pollution.' Tshepo's dad.

At School

Under the Apartheid laws, black and white children had to go to separate schools. Now that the system is over schools are mixed.

Tshepo goes to Itemogele Primary School. There are 45 children in his class.

School starts at 8 o'clock and finishes at 2 o'clock in the afternoon. There are no school lunches so Tshepo's mum makes him sandwiches.

▲ *Tshepo and his friends run to make sure they are not late for school.*

▼ *Children working together around a computer in a city school.*

20

'We all have to work hard at school. My favourite lessons are maths and art.' Tshepo.

Tshepo learns maths, handwriting, technology, art, science and history. He also learns three languages, English, Afrikaans and Sotho, which is his tribal language.

▼ *Children who go to school in the countryside learn about farming.*

Some parents at Tshepo's school pay for their children to have extra lessons. They want their children to have a good education.

▶ *All schoolchildren wear uniform, although some parents find it difficult to afford.*

'I have quite a lot of homework. Sometimes my mum helps me.' Tshepo.

Spare Time

Many South Africans love to spend time outdoors having barbecues and parties, or playing sport. Rugby, cricket and football are very popular. The South African football team reached the finals of the World Cup in 1998.

In the cities people enjoy going to the cinema and theatre.

▲ *A girl fishes from the pier in Cape Town.*

▶ *City children enjoying a game of street hockey.*

'On most days I play with my best friend after school.' Tshepo.

Looking Ahead

Since 1994 all people in South Africa have been able to vote for who they want to lead them. People are excited about the future and hope that there will be more opportunities for black as well as white people.

▼ *More tourists visit South Africa now that Apartheid has gone.*

'When I am older I want to be a policeman so that I can arrest criminals.' Tshepo.

How to Play Hopscotch

Tshepo and his friends enjoy playing hopscotch. They draw a hopscotch plan on the ground with chalk and number the squares from 1 to 10.

- First, throw a stone into square 1.
- Hop over square 1 into square 2.
- Hop into squares 3 and 4, landing with one foot in each.
- Then jump into square 5, hop into squares 6 and 7, jump into square 8, and hop into squares 9 and 10.
- Then jump completely around and land in squares 9 and 10, facing the way you have come.
- Jump and hop back again in the same way, stopping on square 2.
- Standing on one leg, pick up the stone from square 1 and hop over it.
- Start again, this time throwing the stone into square 2, then square 3 and so on.

▲ *There are different ways to draw out hopscotch plans. This is one of them.*

- You miss a turn if:

(a) your stone does not land in the right square

(b) you accidentally step into the same square as the stone.

The winner is the first person to pick up the stone from square 10 and get back to the start.

◀ *Tshepo must not step in the square with the stone. He hops over it.*

28

South Africa Fact File

◀ Money Facts

South African money is the Rand. There are 100 cents in one Rand.

Independence Day

South Africa has a national holiday on 31 May which is Independence Day. This is the day when all South Africans were able to vote for the first time.

◀ Flag and Anthem

After Apartheid, South Africa had a new flag and new national anthem 'God Bless Africa'. The six colours of the flag include the colours of all the political parties in South Africa.

River Facts

The longest river in South Africa is the Orange River. It is 2,090 kilometres long.

Nelson Mandela

The most famous South African is Nelson Mandela. He spent 27 years in prison before becoming South Africa's first democratically elected president in 1994.

▶ National Park

The Kruger National Park is the largest game park in South Africa. It is almost 20,000 square kilometres. It was founded in 1926 and contains hundreds of different kinds of animals.

World's Largest Diamond

The largest diamond in the world was found in South Africa in 1905. It weighed 0.62 kg It was cut into 105 smaller gems. To find 3 tonnes of diamonds, 30 million tonnes of earth have to be dug out of the ground.

▼ Stamps

Many South African stamps show pictures of their wonderful wild animals.

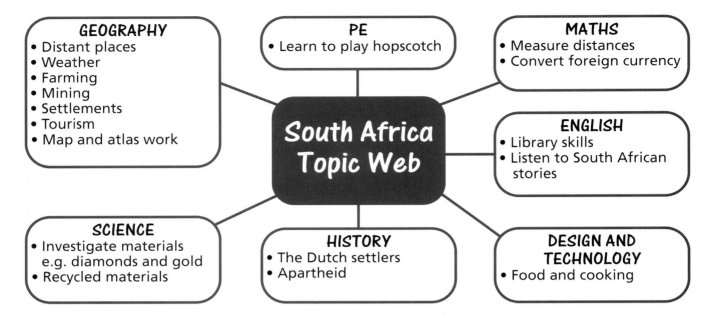

Extension Activities

GEOGRAPHY
- Find South Africa and Britain on a map and a globe.
- Describe how you would get from Britain to South Africa – which countries might you see on the way?

SCIENCE
- Find out about the wild animals that live in South Africa and their habitats.
- Find out how diamonds are used in industry.

HISTORY
- Find out about The Great Trek.
- Imagine you are a settler going to South Africa – make a list of the things you would take with you.

MATHS
- Find out how many Rand there are in one pound. Practise converting the two currencies.
- Using weather data in numerical form, make graphs to show temperature and rainfall figures for South Africa and Britain and compare them.

ENGLISH
- Pretend you are visiting South Africa and write a postcard home.
- Make a list of questions you would ask Nelson Mandela if you met him.

LITERACY HOUR
- Use this book as an example of non-fiction, the story of Nelson Mandela as biography and a story from South Africa as fiction from another culture.

DESIGN AND TECHNOLOGY
- Make Tshepo's favourite food, porridge.
- Design and make a recipe card for porridge.

ART
- Make a collage wildlife poster, advertising the Kruger National Park.

MUSIC
- Listen to songs from South Africa e.g. Ladysmith Black Mombosa Band.
- Listen to the new South African national anthem and anthems from other countries.

INFORMATION TECHNOLOGY
- Find out more information about South Africa from the Internet.

Glossary

Afrikaans The language spoken by Afrikaners, the descendants of Dutch settlers.

Apartheid The system that kept black and white people apart.

Democracy This is where a government has been freely elected by all the adult people.

Desert A place where it hardly ever rains and very few plants can grow.

Game Parks Special areas of land where wild animals are protected.

Plateau A very large and often flat-topped piece of land.

Recycled materials Materials like metal and glass, used again and again to make different things.

Townships These were separate areas on the edges of large cities where black people had to live during Apartheid.

Tribal languages The languages spoken by different groups of African people.

Further Information

Information Books:

Worldfocus: South Africa by John Barraclough (Heinemann, 1996)

Freedom Song: The Story of Nelson Mandela by Neil Tonge (Hodder Wayland, 2002)

One Child One Seed by Kathryn Cave (Frances Lincoln, 2003)

Fiction:

*__At the Crossroads__ by Rachel Isadora (Red Fox, 1993)

*__Charlie's House__ by Reviva Schermbrucker (Walker, 1992)

Journey to Jo'burg: A South African Story by Beverley Naidoo (Collins, 1999)

A South African Night by Rachel Isadora (William Morrow, 1999)

Over the Green Hills by Rachel Isadora (Red Fox, 1995)

* These books are out of print but you may find them in your library.

Useful Address:

South African High Commission, Trafalgar Square, London WC2N 5DP. Tel: 0207 451 7299

Index

All the numbers in **bold** refer to photographs.